PROJECT 17:17

My friend is
struggling with

FINDING

true love

PROJECT 17:17

My friend is struggling with

FINDING

true love

Josh
McDowell
&
Ed Stewart

CF4·K

Finding True Love ISBN: 978-1-84550-356-7
© 2000 Josh McDowell and Ed Stewart
First published by Josh McDowell Ministries in 2000
www.josh.org
This edition published in 2008 by Christian Focus
Publications, Geanies House, Fearn, Tain, Ross-shire,
IV20 1TW, Great Britain. www.christianfocus.com

Cover design by: Daniel van Straaten

Printed by Nørhaven Paperback A/S

Scripture quotations used in this book are from the
Holy Bible, New International Version. Copyright ©
1973, 1978, 1984, International Bible Society. Used by
permission of Zondervan Bible Publishers.

Themes: Romance; Love; Youth-Conduct; Interpersonal
relations; Christian life.

We would like to thank the following people:

David Ferguson, director of Intimate Life Ministries of Austin, Texas, has made a tremendous contribution to this collection.

Dave Bellis, my (Josh) associate of twenty-three years, labored with us to mold and shape each book in this collection. Each fictional story in all eight books in the PROJECT 911 collection was derived from the dramatic audio segments of the "Youth in Crisis Resource," which Dave personally wrote. We are so very grateful for Dave's talents and involvement.

Joey Paul of Word Publishing not only believed in this entire project, but also consistently championed it throughout Word.

Project Partners:

Christian Focus Publications
Geanies House
Fear, Tain, Ross-shire
IV20 1TW, Scotland, U.K.
www.christianfocus.com

Josh McDowell Ministry
P.O. Box 131000
Dallas, TX 75313-1000
U.S.A.

Agapé
Fairgate House, Kings Road
Tyseley, Birmingham B11 2AA
Telephone 0121 765 4404
www.agape.org.uk

CONTENTS

LUKE'S STORY

L UKE EASED UP ON THE ACCELERATOR a little, even though he was secretly anxious to get to the top of the hill. But he slowed the car because his girlfriend, Traci, seated next to him, was enjoying the night view of the city on the gently winding road to the planetarium. And Luke wanted Traci to enjoy the evening because he knew she would make the date more enjoyable for him later if she was happy.

"Look at this, Traci." Luke motioned to the city lights sparkling out his side window.

Just as he hoped, Traci leaned toward him as far as her seat belt would allow to take in the view. The subtle, sweet fragrance of her hair and skin was delicious. Her left hand touched bare skin at the base of his neck, sending a chill of excitement down his spine. Her right hand rested gently on his thigh. The surge of pleasure tempted him to divert his concentration from the road. But he gripped the wheel determinedly and kept his eyes straight ahead. He didn't want a careless accident to spoil this perfect evening.

"Ooo, it's beautiful, Luke," Traci sang. "Look, you can see the train pulling out of the station down there." Her warm breath brushed his ear, giving him another chill of excitement.

Luke glanced out the window for a half second. "Yeah, that's neat," he said, even though he never saw the train.

"You're so sweet to bring me up here on such a beautiful night," Traci said. Then she nuzzled him on the cheek with her nose, concluding with a soft peck of a kiss before settling back in her seat. Luke could feel his heartbeat quicken at her closeness. Traci always sparked the greatest feelings in him. He couldn't get enough of her – her looks, her smell, and especially her touch. He was almost sure she felt the same way about him.

This had been an expensive evening for Luke.

Traci loved romantic dates, so he had treated her to a candlelight dinner at an expensive French restaurant in town. Since it was kind of a dressy evening, he'd also had to spring for a nice shirt and tie. And the planetarium show at the observatory would cost him another huge chunk of change. As a high school senior with a part-time job, Luke could hardly afford such a costly date.

But when he'd picked up Traci at her house tonight, he'd known the expense was worthwhile. She looked more like a movie star than a high-school junior in a dress that accentuated her drop-dead figure. She was worth every minute of overtime he would put in next week to replenish his wallet.

"Tell me about the planetarium show at the observatory again," Traci cooed, gently caressing Luke's upper leg. "I can't believe I have lived in town almost a year now and have never been up here."

"The planetarium theater has a large, domed ceiling," Luke explained, trying to keep his mind off Traci's hand on his leg. "When the lights are turned off, a special projector fills the dome with specks of light. It looks just like the sky at midnight, full of stars and planets. The narrator points out the major stars and constellations. There are asteroids and shooting stars. It's really cool."

"I love astronomy. I can't wait," Traci said with a cute little laugh. "The stars are so romantic." Luke smiled to himself. As long as Traci felt romantic, he was sure to have a good time.

It was chilly on top of the hill, so Luke wrapped his arm around Traci as they hurried from the parking lot to the planetarium theater. There were at least two hundred people watching the program, Luke figured, but he noticed no one but Traci. She seemed to enjoy the presentation, and Luke enjoyed being close to her, relishing the softness of her hand in his. Encouraged by her closeness, he stole an occasional kiss in the darkness, and Traci responded warmly.

After the show, they strolled to a bench outside where they could see the city lights. Luke draped his jacket around Traci's shoulder and wrapped her in his arms. Alone on the bench, huddled with Traci to stay warm, Luke's desire for her heated up. Her willingness spurring him on, Luke's kisses became more passionate than ever before. The pleasure was intense, and he just wanted to be closer to her. Traci's response told him she wanted the same thing.

Once they returned to the car and resumed their romantic cuddling, Luke could hardly keep himself under control. As a Christian, he understood the importance of sexual purity. He had promised God at youth camp three years before that he would remain a virgin until he was married, and he had kept his promise through high school. But his vow had never really been tested until he'd met Traci Lockhart two months earlier. His feelings for her were so strong, not like anything he had felt for other girls. It was a hunger that just seemed to grow more intense with every date.

Swept up in the emotion of the moment, Luke smothered Traci with kisses. Yielding to the urgency he sensed, he touched and caressed her in ways he never had before. Traci seemed so willing, so receptive to the affection Luke yearned to shower on her. It took all the willpower he could muster to stop before breaking his promise to God. "We had better get home," he said, pulling away from her reluctantly.

"Yeah, I guess so," Traci said timidly.

They drove home in silence. Luke felt embarrassed for being so bold in his physical approach to Traci, but he seemed almost driven. Why did he feel more strongly toward Traci than any other girl he'd dated? Why did he feel so compelled to have sex with her?

Finding True Love

As he drove down the hill toward the city, the thought occurred to him for the first time: My desire for Traci is so strong, I must really be in love with her.

TRACI'S STORY

TRACI PRAYED TO GOD SILENTLY AS Luke drove her home. "Forgive me, God, for compromising my standards." She was ashamed of her behavior, seemingly on the verge of breaking her vow of purity to God. Traci had never intended to go all the way with Luke or any other boy before marriage. But she had been swept away by her emotions tonight. The romantic dinner, the candles, the stars, Luke's eagerness to make her feel special – everything seemed so right. He had been so sweet and affectionate to her, she would have done anything to please him.

Then, for some reason, Luke stopped before it was too late. Traci was very relieved, but she was also a little disappointed. He was so abrupt that she wondered now if she had done something wrong.

Did he stop because I was too willing? Was I not willing enough? Did I do something that turned him off? Was he disappointed because I didn't measure up to other girls he has been with?

These questions nagged at Traci during the silent ride home. She hoped this would not be their last time together; she did not want to lose this great guy. Traci remembered their first meeting – at a weekend ski retreat for the high-school group from the church Luke attended. Traci, who went to a much smaller church across town, signed up at the invitation of Polly, a friend from school who attended Luke's church. Traci had noticed Luke as soon as she'd arrived at the church. He was a leader in the high-school group, welcoming students at the registration table in the parking lot and handing out bus and cabin assignments. Luke was not only nice to her, a first-time visitor; he was nice to everyone and working hard to get the retreat off to a positive start. And he was too cute for words!

Traci was quietly elated when Luke ended up on her bus, sitting only a couple of rows away. During the three-hour drive up the mountain, Traci's attention was divided between chatting with Polly and her friends and secretly watching Luke and his friends, who were having even more fun. Traci admired from a distance his wit and humor, and she was impressed with his respect for the adult leaders and his ability to help everyone have a good time. He led their bus load of students in prayer for travel safety and for spiritual and relational growth during the retreat. This was a quality Christian guy, Traci realized, and she wanted to get to know him better.

The weekend afforded so many "unplanned" opportunities to get acquainted that Traci suspected Luke may have noticed her too. He and his friend Curtis showed up at her breakfast table Saturday morning. While Curtis kept Polly occupied, Luke peppered her with questions:

How did you find out about our church and the retreat? What is your church like? How long have you been a Christian? How long have you been skiing? What do you plan to do after high school?

It was obvious Luke was not like most of the guys she knew. He asked questions about her instead of bragging about himself or trying to impress her with his macho accomplishments. He was interested in her spiritual life. He was courteous, and he actually had table manners. Before that weekend, Traci had never before met an eighteen-year-old boy she considered a gentleman. She ate her breakfast slowly because she did not want their first conversation to end.

That afternoon on the slopes, Traci encountered Luke several times. He was a good skier and she was not, so he offered a few helpful pointers, without embarrassing her for her limited ability and experience. Luke happened along a few times when Traci fell, helping her up and making sure she was not hurt. And that afternoon in the lodge, he appeared with a cup of steaming hot chocolate as she sat by the fire drying her socks and warming her feet. She was bothered that the strange numbness in her hands had flared up again, but she didn't mention it to Luke. They talked for more than an hour, time Luke could have spent skiing. Traci was enthralled. Luke was so kind, so sweet, so polite, so helpful. She could not believe he was paying attention to her when practically any girl on the mountain would have jumped at the chance to be with him.

Preparing for the Saturday night bus ride home, Traci arranged to leave the seat next to her empty, hoping Luke would sit there when he was finished with the announcements and prayer. He did, and

Traci was secretly ecstatic. They talked for three hours, while most of the kids on the bus slept. They shared with each other how they came to Christ, their dreams for the future, their favorite foods, movies and music. Traci couldn't believe how much they had in common. Just before they pulled into the church parking lot, Luke asked her out for the next weekend. She accepted immediately, intent on canceling anything on her calendar that might keep her from being with Luke.

The two months from that night to tonight had been magical, Traci assessed. Luke treated her like a princess. Their first date had been a picnic by the lake, with Luke fixing the lunch and providing soft music on his boom box. He took her to movies – the romantic kind she liked instead of car-exploding, gun-blazing guy movies. He took her to a play at the performing arts center. They took long walks downtown and in the country. They laughed and sang and even prayed together. On their third date Luke had kissed Traci for the first time, and she'd stayed awake half the night thinking how special she felt to be his girlfriend.

Luke was ever the perfect gentleman – a real-life Prince Charming. He brought flowers to her. He opened doors for her and seated her at tables. He called; he sent her cards and notes. They kissed and embraced often and held hands most of the time they were together. But Luke had never emphasized the physical side of their relationship – until tonight.

Luke stopped the car in front of Traci's house and, as always, hurried around to her side to open the door. As soon as she stepped out, she was face to face with him in the cool night air.

"Traci, I'm ... I'm sorry about tonight," Luke stammered. "I mean ... I just ... felt so close to you...." His voice trailed off, and Traci knew he was having trouble saying what he meant.

"It's all right, Luke," she said reassuringly. "You're so sweet, I know you didn't mean to do anything wrong. I'm glad we stopped. Thank you."

After several silent seconds he said, "Is it okay if I call you tomorrow?"

Traci smiled. "I was hoping you would." After being kissed lightly on the cheek, Traci went inside. Standing at the window, she watched Luke drive away. Even tonight he was the perfect gentleman, she thought dreamily, apologizing for his passionate advance, asking permission to call me. I forgave him, and I can't wait to talk to him tomorrow. Luke and I have something very special. It must be ... true love.

TIME OUT TO CONSIDER

TRACI AND LUKE HAVE ONLY BEEN dating two months. But the big L-word is already on their minds and no wonder, since we live in a love-crazed culture. Love is the predominant theme in many of our popular songs, movies, novels and TV programs. Everywhere you look in the world of entertainment, someone is either falling into love, falling out of love, making love, faking love, giving love, needing love, living in love or dying for love.

In the real world, life without love is the pits. The yearning to love and be loved by someone is as common in the human family as heartbeat and breath. Everyone seems to crave true love, a love that is strong and deep, a love that will last for all time. Yet the pursuit of love has caused more heartache and pain, more brokenness and bitterness, than all the diseases and wars in history.

What is this thing called love and how do you know when you have found it? People like Traci and Luke are willing to give almost anything to experience love, particularly from the opposite sex. Love makes the world go 'round, we say. Yet many students searching for love find only heartache and disappointment because they don't know what they are looking for. They confuse true love with other experiences and emotions. As a result, they fail to experience love because they don't know what love is and what love isn't.

Perhaps you identify with Traci or Luke. You are in a relationship with someone very special and the L-word is on your mind if not in your vocabulary. Are you "in love"? Do you know how to tell if you are? Or maybe you haven't found that someone special yet, but you want to be ready when you do. You want to know what true love is so you can recognize it when it happens in your life.

The first step to identifying true love is to see what true love isn't.

True love is not the same as lust

Love and lust are often confused in our culture. In fact, many of today's movies, popular songs and novels about love are really about lust. How can you tell the difference? Love gives; lust takes. Love values; lust uses. Love endures; lust subsides.

Luke may be a little confused between the two. He enjoys being close to Traci because she awakens his pleasurable sexual urges and feelings. He does nice things for Traci at least in part because he thinks it will make her more willing to share the physical closeness and intimacy that he enjoys. And his lust nearly caused him to compromise his sexual purity and hers.

Yes, physical attraction is often the spark that eventually ignites into true love. God designed us with the desire and capacity for sexual intimacy. But if your interaction with someone of the opposite sex is based on intense sexual feelings and physical gratification, lust may be playing the role of love in the relationship.

Love is not the same as romance

When Luke and Traci were together, they could almost hear violins playing sweet love music. When they kissed, emotional fireworks went off inside. Whenever Luke spoke sweet words of love and affection or cared for Traci in kind, romantic ways, she felt like a princess. Whenever Traci gazed lovingly into his eyes, Luke felt stronger and more important than anyone else. Candlelight dinners, soft music and starry skies brought on intense romantic feelings in both of them, especially Traci.

Romantic feelings are wonderful in a close male/female relationship. God wired us to experience these feelings in special relationships with the opposite sex. Perhaps you have enjoyed the inner warmth and fireworks of romance in a dating relationship. But the excitement and warmth of romance cannot be equated with love. Romance is a feeling; true love is much more.

True love is not the same as infatuation

Infatuation is a fascination with and intense interest in someone of the opposite sex. You find yourself thinking about that person all day and dreaming about him or her at night. You plan your day around seeing or talking to that special person. Your thoughts may be so preoccupied with that person that you can't concentrate on anything else. Another term for infatuation is puppy love. Puppy love may be real to a puppy, but if the only love you experience is puppy love, you will end up living a dog's life!

When people talk about "falling in love" or "love at first sight," they are usually talking about infatuation. Infatuation left Traci feeling breathless and starry-eyed about Luke. And Luke sometimes felt light-headed and addle-brained being with Traci. Maybe you have experienced similar feelings about someone of the opposite sex. Infatuation is not wrong, but it should not be mistaken for love. Infatuation is usually "me-centered"; love is "others-centered."

True love is not the same as sex

Many students (and many adults as well) confuse the intensity of sexual desire with true love. It happened to Luke after his sexual hunger for Traci nearly caused him to abandon his promise to remain pure. His strong desire to experience sex with her caused him to wonder if his feelings were based on true love. Perhaps you have wondered the same thing about your sexual desires for someone.

Sex as God intended it is not wrong. It was designed by God for procreation and fulfillment within the bounds of marriage. But sex and love are distinct. You can have sex without love and love without sex. Love is a process; sex is an act. Love is learned; sex is instinctive. Love requires constant attention; sex takes no effort. Love takes time to develop and mature; sex needs no time to develop. Love requires emotional and spiritual interaction; sex requires only physical interaction. Love deepens a relationship; sex without love dulls a relationship.

"If love is more than lust, romance, infatuation or sex," you may wonder, "how do I know if I'm in love?" That's the big question, especially when you find yourself attracted to members of the opposite sex and increasingly involved in dating. To answer that question, you need to know more than what true love isn't. You need to understand what true love is.

Just as many people confuse love with lust, romance, infatuation and sex, many are also in the dark about the different kinds of love people express. There are basically three ways of behaving in relationships that people routinely label as "love."

"I love you if . . ."

Qualified love, "if" love, is conditional love. It is given or received only when certain conditions are met.

The only way to get this kind of love is to earn it by performing in an approved way. Some parents love their children if they behave well, if they get good grades or if they act or dress a certain way. Among married or dating couples, love may be withheld if one partner fails to do or be what the other expects. "If" love is basically selfish. It is a bargaining chip offered in exchange for something desired.

Many young women have only experienced the kind of love that says, "I love you if you give me what I want sexually" or "I love you if you have sex with me just this once." Another subtle sexual "if" pressure is found in the common misconception that all dating couples are having sex. The message is, "Since everyone is doing it, you will love me if you do it too." What these girls don't realize is that the love they expect to win from a boy by meeting his sexual demands is only a cheap imitation of love, intended to compromise their character. It cannot satisfy the need for love, and it is never worth the price of sexual compromise. "If" love always has strings attached. As long as certain conditions prevail, the relationship is fine. But when expectations are not met, love is withdrawn. Many marriages break up because they were built on "if" love. When one or both partners fail to perform up to the desired standard, "love" turns to disappointment and resentment.

Luke's "love" for Traci at this point may be largely based on "if" love. As long as Traci makes him feel good, as long as she dresses to please him, as long as she allows him to enjoy her closeness, he is interested in her. But what would happen to Luke's "love" if Traci said, "No more kissing, no more hand holding, and certainly no more intense cuddling in the car"? Would he still want to be with her and spend his hard-earned money to show her a good time?

"If" love is not true love. If you are in a relationship and sense pressure to perform in a certain way to gain the love you desire, the relationship is not governed by true love.

"I love you because ..."

The second kind of love, "because" love, is a close cousin to "if" love. One person loves another because of something he or she is, has or does. Someone may say, "I love you because you are so beautiful" or "I love you because you take good care of me" or "I love you because you make me laugh." Traci may be an example of "because" love, since she is strongly attracted to Luke because he is so sweet, kind and romantic around her.

"Because" love sounds pretty good. Almost everyone appreciates being loved for who they are or what they do. It is certainly preferable to "if" love, which must be constantly earned and requires a lot of effort. Being loved because we are good-looking, witty, kind, wealthy, popular and so on seems much less demanding and conditional than trying to bargain for love.

But what will happen to Traci's love when she meets someone who is sweeter and kinder than Luke? How will she treat Luke if he stops being an impressive youth-group leader or if he cannot afford to take her on romantic dates? If Traci's love is based on what Luke does, it may not survive any negative changes in his role or performance.

'Because' love is not true love. You may find yourself attracted to someone because of his or her personality, position, intelligence, skill or ability. But if your love is not founded on more than what that person appears to be, has or does, it will not last.

"I love you, period."

The third kind of love is love without conditions. This kind of love says, "I love you despite what you may be like deep down inside. I love you no matter what might change about you. You can't do anything to turn off my love. I love you, period!"

"Love, period", is not blind. It can and should know a great deal about the other person. It may be aware of that person's failures, shortcomings and faults. Yet it totally accepts him or her without demanding anything in return. There is no way you can earn this type of love, nor can you lose it. It has no strings attached.

"Love, period", is different from "if" love in that it does not require certain conditions to be met before it is given. It is also different from 'because' love in that it is not generated by attractive or desirable qualities in the other person. Lust, romance, infatuation, sex, "if" love and 'because' love are predominantly about getting something from another person. True love is about giving to another person. Luke and Traci are still closer to the getting side in their relationship. If what they identify as love is to grow into true love, each of them will need to make a transition to the giving side.

LUKE'S STORY

LUKE TUGGED AT THE BILL OF HIS batting helmet and settled his feet into the batter's box. After a couple of practice swings with the aluminum bat, he called out, "Okay, Doug, I'm ready."

Doug Shaw stood outside the batting cage with the coins Luke had given him. At Luke's words, he dropped them into the machine to activate the mechanical pitcher sixty feet from where Luke stood coiled and ready. In a few seconds, it hurled the first baseball toward the center of the strike zone. Luke whipped the bat around to meet it. Thwang! The ball shot to the netting high above the mechanical arm and tumbled harmlessly to the cement floor.

"Nice rip, Luke," Doug called out. "It would have been a double deep in the gap, no question."

Doug Shaw and his wife, Jenny, were the volunteer youth sponsors at the church Luke attended. Doug and Luke had just come from a Saturday morning planning breakfast for student leaders in the high-school ministry. As fans of sports in general and baseball in particular, they tried to get to the batting cages once or twice a month together.

The second pitch streaked toward the plate. Luke's swing barely ticked the ball. He missed the next two pitches completely.

"You're upper cutting, man," Doug said. "Level out your swing. Drive the ball instead of trying to loft it."

Luke grunted his acknowledgment, then connected with the next pitch.

"Great swing – another double," Doug said, clapping his hands.

After they had worked up a sweat taking cuts in the cage, Doug and Luke bought cans of soda and sat down at a nearby picnic table in the sunshine to drink them. Their conversation was punctuated by the clink of baseballs making contact with aluminum bats in the batting cages.

When their discussion of baseball had played out, Doug said, "I notice that you have been spending time with the new girl from Madison High, Traci Lockhart."

Luke studied the top of his can of Dr Pepper. "Yeah, I have," he said, without much expression.

"She seems like a nice girl – very sharp upstairs, very sweet."

Luke nodded. "Traci is really special," he said.

Doug evaluated the response. "You don't sound very enthused. Is everything all right, I mean, with you and Traci?"

Luke blew out a long sigh. "I guess I'm supposed to talk to you about it."

"What do you mean?"

Luke took another drink. "Well, I'm not sure how it's going with Traci and me. I prayed last night that if God wanted me to talk to somebody, you'd ask about Traci. Do you mind if I ask you a few questions?"

"Not at all, Luke," Doug said. "I'm always glad to hear what you have to say, and I'll share what I can."

Luke related his account of meeting Traci during the ski retreat. He explained how he'd assigned himself to Traci's bus just to be near her, and that he'd gone out of his way to talk to her during the weekend. He described a few of their dates and how close he and Traci had become in just two months. Doug, chuckling, complimented Luke on his ambition and ingenuity. Luke smiled.

Then he quickly sobered. Speaking softly and haltingly, he told about taking Traci to the planetarium last weekend. Omitting the embarrassing details, he summarized how close he came to breaking his vow of sexual purity. He admitted that he was wrong to take advantage of Traci as he did. By the time he finished his story, Luke seemed on the verge of crying.

"Luke, I can see that your experience last weekend has caused you a lot of anxiety and concern," Doug said. "I feel that with you, my friend, because I love you. And I'm proud of you for doing the right thing in the end." He added an affectionate but manly pat on the shoulder.

"Thanks," Luke said. "I was pretty sure you would understand."

"So where are you and Traci now?" Doug went on. "Did she break up with you?"

"That's the crazy thing about it," Luke returned. "She was glad we didn't ... you know ... go all the way. But she's not mad at me or blaming me for what happened. We talked on the phone a couple of times this week, and she wants to keep going out – double dates, we both agreed."

"And how do you feel about Traci after your experience?" Doug said.

Luke brushed a fly away from his ear. "I'm not sure how I feel, Doug. I want to ask you about it."

"Fire away."

"I've never had such strong feelings for a girl before," Luke explained. "I just want to be with Traci all the time. When we are together, I want to touch her and kiss her, and those desires almost got me in big trouble last weekend. Does this mean I'm ... in love with Traci?"

"The big L-word," Doug said with a slight smile.

"The word love never crossed my mind with other girls I've dated," Luke explained. "Traci is different. I just want to know if it really is love."

"How do you think a person knows he or she is in love?" Doug asked.

Luke shrugged. "It's some kind of very special feeling, I guess."

"Let me put it another way. What do you think being in love looks like?"

Luke waved at the fly again. "I don't know. Maybe it looks like two people holding hands, going places together ..."

Doug pulled a slim, leather-bound New Testament from the back pocket of his jeans. "When I first met Jenny in college, I would have answered those questions the same way you did," he said, flipping through pages. "I want to read to you two verses that really helped me understand what true love is. They're in Ephesians five, verses twenty-eight and twenty-nine."

Doug found the right page and began to read. "'Husbands ought to love their wives as-'"

"Whoa, hold on, Doug," Luke interrupted. "We're talking about the L-word here, not the M-word. I'm not a husband, and I don't plan to be one soon. Marriage with Traci is not in my vocabulary, at least not yet. I need to figure out if I love her first."

"Relax, my friend," Doug said, laughing. "I'm not

trying to herd you to the altar. I just want you to see God's definition of true love. In these verses, love just happens to be applied to husbands and wives. It works in all relationships."

Luke thought for a moment. "Well, okay," he said at last.

Doug started over. "'Husbands ought to love their wives as their own bodies. He who loves his wife loves himself. After all, no-one ever hated his own body, but he feeds and cares for it, just as Christ does the church.'"

"I thought Christians were supposed to love others more than themselves," Luke said.

"We are to love God more than we love ourselves," Doug clarified. "But according to Christ's Great Commandment in Matthew 22, we are to love our neighbor as we love ourselves. And 'neighbor' includes everyone: parents, brothers and sisters, boyfriend or girlfriend, husband or wife."

"But is it right to love ourselves?" Luke pressed. "I mean, isn't that being kind of self-centered?"

"Paul's not talking about people being selfish or self-centered here," Doug explained. "But we all take care of our own basic needs, like getting enough to eat, getting enough sleep, wearing seat belts and driving carefully, and spending time in the Word to grow. Paul says we should care for the needs of others just as we do for ourselves. In fact, you can tell that love is real when the happiness, health and spiritual growth of another person is as important to you as your own."

Luke cocked his head. "The way you talk about it, love isn't a feeling at all. Love is a way of treating people – caring for them as you do yourself."

Doug nodded. "Strong feelings of attraction – like you describe between you and Traci – are often called love because that's how it's portrayed in movies, TV and music. Good feelings may accompany love, but true love can happen with or without feelings, because love is the activity of caring for a person as you care for yourself."

Luke and Doug talked for another twenty minutes, and Doug led them in a brief prayer. Then Doug left to change clothes and relieve his wife, Jenny, at the quick-print shop they owned and operated together. Luke had to leave too; he'd promised Traci he would take her to buy a battery for her car. Before they parted, Doug issued Luke a specific challenge to apply their discussion in his relationship with Traci. Luke had no idea that Doug's challenge would soon be put to a severe, unexpected test.

TRACI'S STORY

TRACI AND HER MOTHER HAD CRIED off and on since their family doctor's phone call earlier in the morning. Dr. Duncan did not usually talk to patients on Saturday mornings, but today was an exception, he had said.

Traci had seen him on Friday about the occasional, bothersome numbness in her hands. She had thought little of the symptoms, but her mother had made an appointment just to check it out. The doctor had deemed it important to call with his preliminary diagnosis.

"Multiple sclerosis?" Traci said to her mother, who had taken the call from the doctor. "I've heard of it, but what is it?"

Jackie Lockhart fought back tears as she explained. "It's a disease of the central nervous system, honey, attacking the brain and spinal cord. They don't know the cause, and they don't know the cure. Depending on the locality of the disease, it can produce . . . disabilities." Jackie could no longer hold back the tears.

"Disabilities? What disabilities?" Traci had demanded, suddenly feeling very afraid. "Mom, what's wrong with me? What's going to happen to me?"

It took Traci's mother several minutes to get through the explanation, interrupted by moments of tears shared with her daughter. Jackie tried to encourage her – and herself – by stating that the symptoms can come and go, disappearing for months or years at a time. But unless a cure was found or God miraculously intervened, Traci might eventually lose the use of her legs, arms, speech, or other physical abilities. In response to Traci's direct question, Jackie admitted that MS can eventually be fatal.

Drying her eyes, Traci went out to the front porch to wait for Luke. It was so sweet and kind of him to help her buy a car battery. In the meantime, Jackie put in a call to her ex-husband to tell him the bad news. Traci's father lived in another state with his second wife.

Sitting on the porch and staring aimlessly, Traci wondered how Luke would take her news. She had never told him about the numbness in her hands for a couple of reasons. First, until today, the condition was more a bother to her than a worry, so she didn't think it important to mention. Second, Luke was such a great guy, she wanted to do everything she could to impress him. So volunteering information about her "faults" at this early stage of their relationship had seemed unthinkable.

Now she had to tell him. If she didn't, someone else eventually would, and that would be worse. Besides, it was the right thing to do. As much as she feared that the reality of MS might drive Luke away, the only loving thing to do was to tell him. And she did want to do the loving thing with Luke because she was pretty sure she loved him. The question plaguing her as she watched for his car was, Does Luke love me enough to stay with me in spite of what I will tell him? Behind this question was another she did not want to think about at all: Does Luke even love me?

As soon as Luke's car pulled up to the curb, Traci ran to it and jumped in. He noticed her red eyes right away. "You've been crying," Luke said, with obvious concern. "Traci, what's wrong?"

Traci blurted out the news along with another wave of warm tears. She felt very ugly crying in front of Luke, but she couldn't help it. It didn't seem to matter anyway. The fact that she was not very pretty when she cried was minor in light of the fact that she might be crippled some day.

Luke's response was more than Traci could have hoped for. She would not have been surprised if he had backed away from her as if she had leprosy, saying something like, "Have a nice life," and leaving her standing on the curb. After all, a guy as good-looking and sweet as Luke could find a dozen girls without disabilities to go out with by tonight. But instead, he touched her gently and listened intently as she tearfully told him about the disease. He comforted her and encouraged her with caring words. He asked if there was anything he could do for her. And he promised to stick with her through this tough trial.

Then he helped Traci get her feet on the ground again by taking her to the auto parts store to buy the car battery. After installing the battery and giving Traci a tender kiss, he left.

Only later did she begin to wonder if she had seen the last of Luke. Had he been kind, caring and helpful just long enough to make his escape? Was he even now plotting how to extricate himself from this relationship? Or was Luke's concern as genuine as it had seemed? Did he know even more about love than what he had shown her in the past two months?

TIME OUT TO CONSIDER

L UKE WAS BETTER PREPARED TO RECEIVE Traci's startling revelation thanks to a timely visit with his youth sponsor, Doug Shaw. They didn't know it at the time, but the challenge Doug issued to Luke would be put to a severe test the moment Luke arrived at Traci's house.

Doug's challenge was simple enough: Since you are attracted to Traci and she is attracted to you, why not focus your attention on exercising God's definition of love in your relationship?

What is God's definition of love? Love, period, is the only real love, the only true love, the only biblical love. It is the kind of love God displays toward us: unconditional, no if, no because. The Bible declares: "God so loved the world that he gave his one and only Son" (John 3:16); "This is love: not that we loved God, but that he loved us and sent his Son as an atoning sacrifice for our sins" (1 John 4:10); "But God demonstrates his own love for us in this: While we were still sinners, Christ died for us" (Rom. 5:8). This is the God who loves us unconditionally, in spite of our sin, in spite of our weakness.

According to the verses Doug read to Luke outside the batting cages, true, unconditional love is evident when the happiness, health and spiritual growth of another person are as important to you as your own. Paul wrote to the Ephesians, "No one ever hated his own flesh, but nourishes and cherishes it, just as Christ also does the church" (Eph. 5:29 NASB). It is not selfish or self-centered to nourish and cherish our own bodies; it is a natural, healthy love of self. True love means to nourish and cherish another just as we naturally do for ourselves.

To nourish means to nurture toward growth and maturity. For example, to nurture a plant or flower in your garden, you provide all the sun, water and plant food it needs to grow tall and become fruitful. In a similar way, nurturing that special someone in your life means to provide for his or her growth and maturity by meeting needs, just as you make sure your own needs are met.

To cherish means to protect from harm. Picture a mother bird spreading her wings over her babies to shield them from bad weather or danger. Cherishing your special friend means protecting him or her from all harm, just as you take precautions to protect yourself from dangers of any kind.

Here is one of the simplest definitions for true love you will ever find: to protect and to provide for another person. It reflects God's picture of love in the Bible. And the supreme example is Jesus Christ's love for the church. He is alive today, protecting and providing for us.

What does true love look like in a dating relationship? You will speak and act in ways that protect and provide for your boyfriend or girlfriend. For example, you will drive carefully instead of recklessly, because you want to protect your date from an accident. You will provide activities that will be personally enriching and enjoyable for your date instead of those of questionable value. And you will not pressure your date to meet your sexual desires but instead protect him or her from the pain of moral compromise.

As you can see, true love from God's perspective is much more than an attraction to or warm feelings about someone special. True love is a decision, an action, a response to care for others as you do yourself. Protecting and providing for others is an act of the will regardless of our feelings. This is how we are to love everyone: family members, friends, classmates, neighbors, even strangers. We should be constantly seeking the happiness, health and spiritual growth of others, beginning with those closest to us – family members and close friends – and working out to people we don't even know, such as people around the world who benefit from our charitable giving.

If you have a boyfriend or girlfriend, he or she belongs in that inner circle. If you are learning how to protect and to provide for anyone, it should be the one to whom you are most deeply attracted. The relationship may have begun by focusing on infatuation, romantic attachment, or even sex. You may have recognized large doses of I love you if ... or I love you because ... in the way you treat one another. Conditional love rarely protects or provides for another.

If you want the relationship to grow and succeed in God's terms, focus on applying God's definition of love: I love you, period! This unconditional love seeks to protect and provide for the other person. Consciously make your friend's happiness, health and spiritual growth as important to you as your own. If you are in a romantic relationship, you will know it is true love when your heart's desire is to protect and provide for the object of your affection.

Traci's shocking news about MS has sobered Luke and challenged him to re-evaluate their relationship. A few hours after being with Traci, Luke found himself seeking out his spiritual mentors, armed with more questions.

LUKE'S STORY

LUKE SAT IN HIS CAR OUTSIDE THE quick-print shop until almost 6.00 p.m. He approached the door just as Jenny Shaw was coming to lock it and flip the window sign from OPEN to CLOSED. The concern on his face must have been as obvious as a blinking neon sign. "Hi, Luke," Jenny said as he approached the door. "Is something wrong?"

"Can I talk to you and Doug for a minute?" he said.

"Of course, Luke. Come on in." Jenny locked the door behind them and led Luke back to the office where Doug was shutting down a computer.

Luke poured out the story of Traci's recently discovered disease. Doug and Jenny were shocked, saying they would stop by Traci's house on their way home from work.

"I understand a lot more about love since we talked together this morning, Doug," Luke went on. "And I accepted your challenge to begin showing true love to Traci. But I didn't expect this. I mean, Traci is a beautiful girl, but in time her disease could change that. She may not be able to ski or swim or go biking. And if we get married someday – I'm not saying we're going to, but if we do – will she be able to have sex and bear children? I know true love says 'I love you, period,' but I didn't know that period would be so huge."

Doug and Jenny put their hands on their young friend's shoulders. "This has been a tough day for you, Luke," Jenny said, "and we're so sorry about the disappointment you are facing. We will be praying for you as well as for Traci."

"Thanks. That means a lot to me."

Then Doug said, "Only God knows the future, Luke. Only He knows if you and Traci are destined to spend your lives together as husband and wife. That's something you can leave in God's hands, because it's in the future. In the meantime, are you still attracted to Traci, I mean, beyond the physical attraction?"

Luke paused only a moment before answering. "Of course. Traci is a special person. She's fun, smart, happy, and we have so much in common. I admit that her appearance got my attention first. But there is a lot more to Traci than how she looks."

"It sounds like Traci means a lot to you," Jenny put in.

Luke nodded. "Yes, a lot."

"Then you have nothing to lose by making Traci's happiness, health and spiritual growth as important to you as your own. Loving her God's way will make the most of your relationship right now. And if, in God's plan and timing, you and Traci marry someday, your relationship will be based on true love, not an earthly substitute."

Luke pondered the words for several moments. "Okay, but how? Can you give me some practical examples of what my love for Traci can look like, especially in light of what she found out today?"

Doug and Jenny spent the next few minutes offering suggestions. When they all stood to leave, Luke hugged and thanked both of them. He told them he was heading back over to Traci's house for a while. The couple said they would see him there after they got the store buttoned up for the night.

Before leaving the shopping center, Luke stopped at the card shop to buy a card for Traci. He selected one he thought she would like, not a mushy, romantic card, but one with a pretty floral design and blank space inside to write.

He wrote only a few quick lines, knowing there would be many other cards, notes and conversations in the future: "Traci, you are a wonderful person. I know you can get through this trial. I will be here to help you every step of the way." He rolled the pen in his fingers for several seconds before writing the final two words. They had much more significance to him now, so he wrote them with confidence: "Love, Luke."

TIME OUT TO CONSIDER

WHAT DOES TRUE LOVE LOOK LIKE in a boyfriend-girlfriend relationship? It has the same basic elements as love expressed in any other relationship, though elements of affection and time commitment may be greater in this special relationship. Here are a few examples.

Finding True Love

True love seeks to meet needs for comfort, support and encouragement

This was the first thing Doug and Jenny mentioned to Luke when he asked for practical suggestions on showing true love. Everybody needs comfort, support and encouragement, especially during the inevitable times of pain and discouragement in life. Comfort is not a "pep talk," urging another person to hang in there, tough it out, or hold it together. Comfort is not an attempt to explain why bad things happen to people. Comfort is not a bunch of positive words about God being in control and everything being okay. All of these things may be good and useful in time, but they do not fill the primary need for comfort.

People receive comfort when we feel their hurt and sorrow with them so they know they are not suffering alone. Paul instructed us, "Rejoice with those who rejoice; mourn with those who mourn" (Rom. 12:15).

Jenny instructed Luke to comfort Traci and her mother by offering a gentle touch, a tender embrace and a shoulder to cry on. When your special friend is hurting for some reason, share words like, "I know it hurts," "I'm so sorry you have to go through this," or "I really hurt for you."

Save your words of advice or admonitions from Scripture until you have shared your friend's feelings. That's biblical comfort.

True love also meets the need for support

You provide support when you attempt to lighten your friend's load in practical, helpful ways. Acts of support fulfill Paul's instruction in Galatians 6:2: "Carry each other's burdens, and in this way you will fulfill the law of Christ."

Luke may have opportunities to perform a number of helpful tasks for Traci and her mother that will help ease their burden in practical ways. You express biblical love to your special friend whenever you serve him or her in practical, helpful ways.

Everybody needs encouragement in life, and true love looks for ways to meet that need. We encourage others whenever we do or say something thoughtful to lift their spirits. The card Luke is taking to Traci, especially the encouraging words he wrote inside, is a simple way of expressing encouragement. You can supply encouragement to others in many practical ways, such as cards, notes, e-mails or phone calls. Encouragement is communicated when you focus your words and attention on your special friend and any struggles he or she is going through.

Finding True Love

True love does not take advantage of another person

Using someone in a "love" relationship for your own emotional, physical or sexual gratification violates love's guideline of protecting and providing. Taking for your own pleasure does not contribute to the happiness, health and spiritual growth of another person.

True love will not pressure another person into sex

There is tremendous pressure in our culture for students to become sexually active, even in casual dating relationships. Today's movies, music and media treat premarital sex as normal and expected. But sex outside God's plan for intimacy in marriage can leave mental, emotional and spiritual scars for years. True love protects a person from such guilt and pain, and it provides for a secure, nurturing relationship by saying no to premarital sex.

True love will not insist on an "exclusive" friendship

Some students become possessive of a boyfriend's or girlfriend's time and attention which restricts and stifles a person's happiness, health and spiritual growth. True love encourages healthy interaction with others.

True love will not do anything to damage the happiness, health and spiritual growth of another person. So how do you know when you have found true love? You know love is real when you make the happiness, health and spiritual growth of your boyfriend or girlfriend as important to you as your own. That's what it means to protect and provide for someone you love. The following guidelines will help you integrate this definition into your experience with that special person in your life.

- Put Jesus Christ first in your relationship.

- Be open and honest with each other.

- Accept each other completely, including faults and failures.

- Seek your parents' approval for your relationship.

- Avoid any setting or activity that may tempt you to compromise your commitment to sexual purity.

- Handle disagreements quickly and lovingly.

- Emphasize the "friend" in boyfriend and girlfriend.

It's too soon to tell if Luke and Traci's relationship will develop into a marriage commitment. Many other factors will come into play over the next months and years, particularly God's leading in their college and career decisions. But Luke has turned a corner in his relationship with Traci.

He has accepted Doug's challenge to protect and provide for her as long as they are together. This is a no-lose situation for both of them. If Luke and Traci end up getting married in the future, they will begin their life together on the solid foundation of protecting and providing for each other, which is God's kind of love. If they should eventually go their separate ways, they can part with no regrets, having contributed to each other's health, happiness and spiritual growth.

You may be no more certain about the future with your special friend than Luke and Traci are about theirs. But the prospects for your relationship will be just as bright and positive as you focus on the true love of protecting and providing for one another.

Titles in this series:

978-1-84550-354-3
My Friend is Struggling with
Conflicts with Others

978-1-84550-355-0
My Friend is Struggling with
The Death of a Loved One

978-1-84550-356-7
My Friend is Struggling with
Finding True Love

978-1-84550-357-4
My Friend is Struggling with
Thoughts of Suicide

ABOUT THE AUTHORS

JOSH MCDOWELL is an internationally known speaker, author and traveling representative of Campus Crusade for Christ, International. He has authored or co-authored more than fifty books, including *Right from Wrong* and *Josh McDowell's Handbook on Counseling Youth*. Josh and his wife, Dottie, have four children and live in Dallas, Texas.

ED STEWART is the author or co-author of numerous Christian books. A veteran writer, Ed Stewart began writing fiction for youth as a co-author with Josh McDowell. He has since authored four suspense novels for adults. Ed and his wife, Carol, live in Hillsboro, Oregon. They have two grown children and four grandchildren.

CHRISTIAN FOCUS PUBLICATIONS

Christian Focus | Christian Heritage | CF4K | Mentor

Christian Focus Publications publishes books for adults and children under its four main imprints: Christian Focus, CF4K, Mentor and Christian Heritage. Our books reflect that God's word is reliable and Jesus is the way to know him, and live for ever with him.

Our children's publication list includes a Sunday School curriculum that covers pre-school to early teens; puzzle and activity books. We also publish personal and family devotional titles, biographies and inspirational stories that children will love.

If you are looking for quality Bible teaching for children then we have an excellent range of Bible story and age specific theological books.

From pre-school to teenage fiction, we have it covered!

Find us at our web page:
www.christianfocus.com

CF4•K
Because you're never
too young to know Jesus